Beyond the Ceiling

A Fresh Perspective for Winning!

PATRICK O. OTUOMA

WESTBOW® PRESS
A DIVISION OF THOMAS NELSON & ZONDERVAN

Scripture taken from the King James Version of the Bible.

WestBow Press books may be ordered through
booksellers or by contacting:

WestBow Press
A Division of Thomas Nelson & Zondervan
1663 Liberty Drive
Bloomington, IN 47403
www.westbowpress.com
1 (866) 928-1240

ISBN: 978-1-4908-7103-5 (sc)

Library of Congress Control Number: 2015902936

Print information available on the last page.

WestBow Press rev. date: 02/23/2015

CONTENTS

This book is dedicated to my mother, Mary Colet who always believed in me. Your inspiration made this book possible!

PREFACE

> "Everyone's got a sun opportunity; even so, affection for the sunrise or sunset is a personal choice!"
>
> *-Patrick Otieno Otuoma*

There lies a huge measure of limitation under our ornamented ceiling covers! Right from the designated partitions all the way to the spatial restrictions, you are certain to find borders all around you. In spite of these confines however, there exists a new frontier- one free of boundaries; it is just beyond the apparent ceiling cover!

Could your embers of success be super heated, yet dormant? Or, might your personal best require some bit of revving? Certainly! - As your clearest chance to achieving the successes you very much desire.

The society we live in has abruptly shifted gears into overdrive. It is presently not just reserving exclusive facilities for 'members only', but also exposing 'non members' to untold devastation. Quite often, outcomes are constantly influenced by resources and the influences thereof. Result is- underachievement presents fewer or no alternatives to remedy.

Fate has devised a formula for forcing individuals to the niches of insignificance. By this, it has confined folks to the wheelchairs of repressiveness. It is against this background that this book was conceived; as a clarion call to each of us to make the vital steps in confronting the upheavals that grace our sojourns.

You have faced off with improbable giants. Yes, you have! Some of the times, your ventures have crashed hopelessly. The world has mostly looked away at your ordeals. Potentially, every chance for growth has been dwarfed by constant resistances.

The world's view has rubbed you the wrong way, who knows! And your only chance resigned to a very critical position, where you've got to tackle your critics on the break. I've been there before, and I've got news for you! Your time is now. So, make your productivity count for something worthwhile. Do not write your epitaph yet. There's much more to fight for.

Perfection is realized through selflessness and effort. It therefore calls upon you to turn your doubts into gushing torrents of power, speed, hope, passion, possibility and belief. It does not matter that you are the average kid on the block. What matters is your resolve to strike it big in your pursuits.

It is about time you tuned to the right voices- those that speak affirmation and encouragement- the ones that tell you 'yes, you can!' The voices that urge you to do the kind of things you are best at without apologies. That is the kind of charm required to get over the board, and provoke your critics to brand you 'a little lucky'

With such determination to win, and desperation never to lose, your turning point is a short while away.

INTRODUCTION

> "A man's gift makes room for him, and brings him before great men"
> (Proverbs 18:16 The King James 2000 Version)

Turning around is not a mere walk in the park, neither a birthday wish for our insatiable appetites. No! Turning around is a U-Turn moment where resolve may be flipped against the oncoming traffic. It is what may cause your unique gift to count for something worthwhile.

In the pursuit of success, such turns are pricey. The minute you realize that your route is ill conceived and that you're headed into the wrong direction, you're at liberty to turn around into the opposite direction.

Sharing my experiences with folks has not only strengthened my conviction that our stories are common, but also that our struggles never go to waste. We face the same monsters, same frustrations, and common foes.

Some times back, I met a Nairobi based author. So enthusiastic was David Waweru as he traced his account and journey of life. Every so often, I beamed in resonance with our 'common pattern' of youthful experience.

Though born and raised hundreds of miles apart, we shared a lot of parallels between us. Our generational differences were less important then, what ran deep were the similarities of the giants we had to vanquish.

In spite of these giants- big or small, your destination must always be defined. Everybody's vision must always settle at their crested hill tops, where nerve and resolve meet.

In her acceptance speech, the Kenyan Oscar winner Lupita Nyong'o underpinned the magic of belief with her famous line, 'No matter where you come from, your dreams are as valid.'

It is not money- but vision that you badly need to make a genuine turn around. Physical challenges such as blindness have no business defining any of us. In such cases, opportunity, rather than pity must be given a chance to thrive.

A JOURNEY OF SUCCESS

"I can do all things through Christ who strengthens me."

(Phil 4:13 KJV 2000)

The human brain packs the greatest resource deposits of all time and no microchip may easily rival it. The intellect will never suffer obsolesce on account of information age; neither will it be swept aside by the persistence of technological advancement.

Looking at the developments of this century, or perhaps the last one, summed together and documented, I am fully persuaded that no man will ever invent anything superior to the human brain- a creation of the Almighty himself.

Every person is endowed, so amazingly with abilities and talents adequate to keep them accelerating. Education is propitious for success. Nevertheless, it is not the only avenue to success. It is therefore incumbent that every individual refines themselves in spite of their formal education to exploit their God-sized potentials.

Every so often, our stages are always before us- set and ready. The biggest tragedy is our failure to realize them, and the fact that they lie idle waiting for our taking. Legends are not carved out of granite. No, they are made of flesh and ride on the wave of inspiration.

So, if the brain is that rich and so prolific, do we ideally exhaust its opulence and resources? There are amazing dynamites contained in the cells of this natural gem called 'brain'. These gems must be fully utilized.

The world has offered great avenues for expression, especially after two ravaging world wars; chief among these in sports, music, and the theatre. You've got a place in this planet to be heard in your unique way- big or small.

THE FACES OF FAILURE, SUCCESS

"For His anger endures but for a moment;
in His favor is life: weeping may endure
for a night, but joy comes in the morning"
(Psa 30:5 KJV 2000)

Have you any experiences with failure, fond or otherwise? How about success? Which of these has befallen you the most? The jury is about out on this sizzling question and statistics are clearly stubborn. Failure has claimed a lion share this time around.

While success is slow and clumsy, failure brandishes its hitherto aggressive ego and has no apologies for its characteristic bravado. If these two landed a slot in a kindergarten, failure would be the smarter one- thanks to hype. I dare say success acts slow and sluggish.

Your personal story might just take cue. Take a brief moment and with eyes closed, run a quick flashback on your encounters. You probably will unearth those moments of nerve and sweat. Seasons when your decisions were never entirely the best and you finally found the courage to admit failure.

'Who's a failure therefore?' No! According to me, it's unlikely that a person should fit that bill for the obvious reason that both success and failure form part of an individual's experiences every so often. Failure represents a state.

In my view, it's an eventual destination that a person may get to, depending on the circumstances that dictate their orientation. In other words, success and failure are but two sides of the same coin-the coin as a hypothetic portrait of an activity carried out by an individual or a group. The chances of either of the occurrences depend on a number of biases. These biases are the prevailing circumstances that influence the outcome of a toss.

An unbiased coin has pretty much equal chance of falling on its either side, say tail or face- in which case either success or failure may result. Biasing the coin however offers a chance of tilting outcomes. This biasing must be done to correspond to the desired results.

An individual's propensity to succeed is tied to a number of varying factors, like in the coin analogy. Failure may also result from an inability to match preparedness with opportunity. Quite often, a person shows up late and misses the opportunity for their desired break.

In essence, your capacity to succeed might be lying in a state of subdue and inertia. Else put, success in slumber land- waiting to be roused. Success is a progression, and not an overnight break.

Our destinations are usually influenced by the biasing we apply -what I refer to as the moment of critical decision making. To squeeze out success, it is only quintessential that an emphatic bias is applied to the influencing factors. That's what it takes to enhance the probability of success.

If an interview were conducted on why failure occurred, there's a likelihood that numerous propositions would be on offer. Up till now, none of us has invited failure, yet it has crashed into our bash across town. It has mastered the art of self invitation, and promptly shrugs orders of restraint.

Like an astrologer, failure has mastered the art of soul searching. It knows impeccably when invitations are made, subtle as they may appear. It also knows when intentions are not backed by firm resolutions- a character that makes it pass as a cunning palm reader.

Before you know it, failure has become your guest with the slightest show of tolerance, when your door is unsecured. And lo and behold, with you is an abiding guest at breakfast through dinner.

Success doesn't stoop that low. On the contrary, it must be guided in, and entertained to feel at home. You may occasionally flog it, drag it and wheel it in to be a little assured of it. If you do not put a keen eye on it, it sneaks out and must thereafter be persuaded back in.

I have since childhood had a penchant for birds. Over time, I reared a rare chicken breed- a gift for stellar performance in my school year's final exams. The bird was spotless, white and very much friendly. What a unique showing for an ordinary bird! Each market day, I sampled rare fish worms and cereals, and as usual, kept my pet fowl conveniently nourished.

After a while, the hen laid eggs and began brooding over them. The startling eggs drew an amount of interest, typical of the discovery era that marked my world. What seemed improbable was the urgency with which the chicks disembarked from their tight compartments. The little chicks sneakily trained their tender beaks to crack their shells and earn their deserved freedoms.

That is the attitude of success! It is an attitude that calls upon each of us to train their beaks to pound away the obstacles that form a shell around our dreams. So, keep pecking incessantly! Yes, until the shell gives way.

IMPERATIVES TO SUCCESS

Success would make the choicest island destination for any sojourner out to splash their hard earned fortune. The only question that would most certainly beg would be- how to land on the shores of this beautiful island. There is no shortage of guide tracts readily on offer and it takes the genuinely prepared to find their way round. Otherwise, the result would be a pathetic cul-de-sac.

CHAPTER 1

Regain your Lost Confidence

Confidence begets confidence and is usually hard earned. The last time I checked, it was the one item you could not have purchased from a provision store. Confidence has a magnetic boomerang which attracts a response every time it is given. It is every conman's talisman. You seldom earn confidence without first giving it.

Before a con is attempted, a conman has to project confidence and hope it reverts back. If returned, then a con is likely to result. You may have noticed that confidence is a prominent requirement for a sales job. If you hope for such an assignment, you have no excuses but to pump it up in your veins.

Confidence doesn't belong to the closet or trophy cabinet. Real, palpable confidence is never locked up. It is a feeling of control that shows up every time a corrective action is needed. You can't profess confidence and keep your dissenting views to yourself.

Leadership is one mission impossible without confidence. Before He mandated Joshua, God commanded him to be strong and of good courage. With confidence, an individual transcends the affairs of self and becomes an advocate for the feeble and a voice for the voiceless.

History is replete with accounts of great leaders who demonstrated exceptional leadership; thanks to their matchless confidence. Mahatma Gandhi stood for the oppressed Indians and earned his place in the roll of honor. His demonstration of confidence earned him accolades.

Martin Luther King junior did not simply win a Nobel. To date, he remains second youngest ever to receive the commendation and went ahead to seal his name in the annals of history. Americans to date observe a holiday to honor Martin Luther King Day. Through the civil rights movement, King unequivocally made his robust brand of advocacy to count.

Confidence is contagious and is often transmitted from person to person. Your confidence or lack of it is able to rub on those you interact with. Like flu, it is contracted without breaking a sweat. I have interacted with individuals whose company has either eroded or otherwise reinforced my confidence, and that is how close it can get.

You must therefore select your company so carefully lest your confidence ship capsizes. Constant practice and exercise builds the fibre of confidence. The moment you start acting confidently, a remarkable improvement kicks in and grows into bank-bursting torrents.

Laughter is often described as the best medicine especially in situations that would otherwise be unsightly. It dilutes the face of anguish and grimace. Laughter sets wheels on the confidence wagon. Whenever failure sneaks its head- and it does often, just laugh the situation off.

During my teenage years, I had a speaking difficulty accentuated by fear and resentment. I perennially got struck by an abnormal shiver that left me speechless. Coherence became virtually impossible. As a consequence, I all but slithered over words as most people would when overcome with fear.

To grow in speech confidence, your first step is to find an audience. If you are people-shy, then turn yourself into an audience and address your image reflected off a mirror. Your image should pretty much suffice as your maiden audience at the outset. Stroll into an empty auditorium and speak to the imaginary audiences. Make a point of fielding questions from the 'audience'. These maneuvers should go a long way in building your confidence and self esteem.

In my own experience, I took time speaking to imaginary audiences, regularly correcting my flaws and learning to manage my breathing. Little by little, I mastered my phobia and honed my skill in public speaking. A situation which initially seemed improbable set up an acumen that has seen me grow more confident.

Driving on Nairobi's Haille- Selassie Avenue on a chilly December, 2012 became tricky by the developments that soon followed. The traffic officer manning the Tom Mboya roundabout had by now got notorious for flagging down motorists for an assortment of traffic offences.

Becoming apprehended was not to me a cause for worry but the astronomical fines slapped on offenders. The weather was anything but impressive on the day, with a little drizzle dampening the morning. As I maneuvered the roundabout, I noticed that the bespectacled cop was keen to have me on the defensive.

His left arm shot in the air, and with his right, he motioned me to park on the outer lane near his BMW bike. Quite clearly, I was on the second lane rightly heading for the exit. From my quick viewpoint, the law enforcer was clearly a no nonsense guy with a slight build.

With his khaki chinos tucked in his boots, he was out to make a kill no matter what. After all, the fines set to curb the traffic chaos were the highest in the world at the time.

Quite frankly, confidence resurges from the determination to stand by what you believe in.

The cop's insistences that I had changed lanes on the roundabout were summarily refuted by me. I rejected those claims with the nerve it deserved. He then ordered me to drive to the famed 'Mlimani' courthouse in his company but still, I grew more hesitant. Looking straight at the cop, I invited him to a contest, and challenged him to simulate a move similar to the one he accused me of- From the innermost lane, to drive and park at the same spot that I had parked the car. My assurance to him was that should he succeed, I'd own up to the offence at once.

Dumbstruck, the cop retreated to consult with his colleagues a short walk away. I was obviously struck by how I conjured such a counter in the heart of the capital, where similar situations had mostly ended with motorists being slapped with hefty fines.

When he returned, the cop asked me to drive away. With no dime to my name and driving a borrowed car, I had confidence to thank for my breaking free.

REMEMBER

- ⊕ Confidence begets Confidence
- ⊕ Confidence can never be locked up
- ⊕ Confidence transcends affairs of self and grants advocacy to the voiceless
- ⊕ Confidence is contagious and is often passed from person to another
- ⊕ Constant practice builds the fibre of Confidence
- ⊕ To grow in confidence, the first step is to find an audience
- ⊕ Confidence resurges from the determination to stand by what you believe in.

Preparedness does the trick

In the pursuit of success, preparedness counts for so much. It's quite inconceivable that a mason should report for duty without his tools of trade. Similarly, it would betray medical code that a GP should operate a clinic without a stethoscope. Such a medic in my opinion would be in an awkward position and might just be ruled out of order.

Betrayal of self worth is when you fail to represent readiness of character as bequeathed by training. When you have adequate preparation, you would never be caught off your guard.

Every action must be matched with initial preparation. Such is only evidenced when the cuffs are off; the hoe firm in hand, stethoscope around the collar and the piece of chalk in your grip.

Opportunity rewards the prepared. It is with such a sense of readiness that dreams become realities. Adequate preparation is vital in spite of the uncertainties surrounding your window of opportunity. This is also true when preparing for an examination.

I can vividly recollect the examination experiences on campus. In such moments, inadequate preparation brought paranoia and a net loss of concentration. Haphazard flipping of pages began in earnest, as everybody scampered to grasp slippery concepts.

Still, there are those who raised the white flag and withdrew. Staring at the tomes and dozens yet to be covered was sufficient to catalyze the reaction called discouragement. Obviously, there was enough reason to lose faith in the face of such uncertainties.

Occasionally, I too ceased preparation due to similar uncertainties. My trepidation with the hurriedly covered content was sufficient to stop the 'waste of time'. In any case, preparation should progress in spite of presenting doubts. Better still, it is always ideal to plan and wait for an opportunity to come by.

Preparation minus action is a venture in futility. There must be redemption at the maturity of preparation. In other words, there comes a logical end to preparation, whereupon execution of assignments begins. It is pointless to prepare forever.

I once stumbled upon a comedy show whose theme matched the subject, 'preparation minus execution'. In the show, the curtains opened on a village bully, seething with venomous bravado, and literally challenging opponents to whichever physical contest he pleased. Having hit his tipping point, some cunning villagers set up a more robust challenge for this homey.

With a wooden piece upon two supports, his assignment was brief- to break the plinth by means of his bare arms. As usual, the rascal unbuttoned his shirt and began flexing his muscles. Next, his vest gave way to more flexing. As though these weren't sufficient, he rid himself of his clumsy belt.

All the while, his challengers cheered him on. After his belt, he rid himself of his trouser, then his shoes. After the shoes, he performed some ritual push- ups. When he was done with this meticulous preparation, he burst into hysterical sobs for his inability to strike the piece of wood. In spite of his grandiose preparation, he lacked the tenacity to take action.

How often do you draft a script that you will fall short of submitting? How about a speech that you will not read? How many times do you paraphrase a question that you will not ask, or plan a conversation that you will not have guts to spark?

There is much to preparation than meets the eye. At the maturity of preparation is a stage called execution. Execution is committing to action that which has been plotted, planned and organized. Essentially, execution is the nerve centre of preparation. Hesitation will never add value to endeavors at all, execution does however.

REMEMBER

- ⊕ Readiness of Character is bequeathed by initial training
- ⊕ Opportunity rewards the Prepared

- ⊕ To draft your Plan and Wait for Opportunity to present
- ⊕ Preparation minus action is a venture in futility
- ⊕ Hesitation will never add value to endeavors at all

Patience Pays...Sure it does

An impending collapse is often announced by the onset of weariness. Before a siege is announced, a feeling of lethargy must have set in amongst the custodians. Weariness is the inability to sustain activity. This lack of persistence is an indication that collapse is imminent. Deficiency of persistence is due to a general loss of patience.

Patience is a virtue without which fruits never ripen. Every tree with a penchant for sweet fruits must learn the virtue of patience. It is the genius of time that matures the acid of a fruit into sweetness, and gives it the sugary taste. It is this Midas touch that turns the novice into an expert, the armature into professional and a rook into champion.

In the area of investments, effort is a vertical component. The horizontal component called time is of unrivalled importance. It pays so well to keep on keeping on, for in a matter of time, sprouting must certainly begin.

In his journey to the U.S presidency, Abraham Lincoln poignantly demonstrated the value of persistence. His sojourn to white house was marked by a myriad of setbacks, each one coming at the heel of the other. His patience never failed him in the presenting tribulations. When everything else deserted Lincoln, his resolve ebbed not in the face of the obvious challenges.

As a matter of fact, every shade of failure was a learning experience and the rushing wind power of his sails. Born in a log cabin on February 12, 1809, Abe did not lose heart with the loss of his mother at a tender age. Performing odd jobs as a farmhand, grocery clerk and much later as a rail splitter, he kept his dreams valid.

Lincoln's failures have often been used to inspire millions of people to overcome difficulties. In 1832, Abraham Lincoln lost his job and failed for the state legislature. The following year, Abe failed in business and in 1835, lost his sweetheart.

In 1836, Abraham Lincoln got a nervous breakdown and two years later in 1838, another defeat for speaker. During the congressional nomination in 1843, Lincoln failed yet again. Five years later in 1848, he lost nomination. In 1849, was rejected for land officer.

As though these were not enough reasons to warrant quitting, in 1854, Lincoln was defeated for U.S Senate. Hot on the heels of his Senate failure was another defeat for vice president. Four years later in 1858, Abe suffered another defeat for U.S Senate.

In the year 1860, Abraham Lincoln was elected the 16th President of the United States of America and sworn into office on March 4, 1861.

Signing my acceptance documents for my undergraduate programme at Kenyatta University gave me an opportunity to undertake Medical Laboratory Science. Later on however, I sought transfer to Nairobi University's College of Architecture and Engineering.

Such transfers were unheard of; thanks to the logistical challenges that were wont to occur around them. Difficult too was the daunting task of engaging the Joint Admissions Board, the universities admissions body.

With the dawn of each day, I kept alive the merit of follow-up. My numerous letters attracted a barrage of unequivocal declines from the admissions board. Most disorienting was a terse reassurance that the position taken by earlier correspondences remained unchanged.

This was a hope killer coming soon after an earlier decline letter. A specially branded envelope lifted my spirit before opening the sealed envelope. The letter headlined "REMINDER". The contents of the letter stipulated succinctly that no vacancies were available for transfer seekers. What a difficult way to start!

Armed with an iconic resolve and a measured yet diligent spirit, I moved from one office to another. I sought to know why the transfer was not possible, considering that faculties had not been filled yet. My presence generated a level of unease that could not be borne for long. It was my cup of tea; to stick to my gun no matter what. My solemn call of duty was to bring this follow-up to its logical conclusion.

One characteristic feature of patience is having an unwavering urge to go on. Patience has a capacity to tolerate delay, trouble, upsets or suffering and still put off the calls to retreat and the urge to surrender. The African Serengeti is one typical example of patience on display.

Watching the African pride of lions stalk prey demonstrates the importance of waiting, and how rewarding it can become. The lion may stalk for very long before a successful pounce, but still, it will stalk. Stalking is synonymous with stealth, and waiting its embodiment. If you must, wait.

In spite of several attempts and rebuttals, it's always a plus to keep on trying especially when others have walked away. Your dreams become reality by constant plying. Let nothing therefore dim your resolve in the wake of improbable outcomes.

REMEMBER

- ✧ The lack of persistence is an indication that collapse is imminent
- ✧ The time component of persistence is of unrivalled importance
- ✧ Patience has a virtue called follow-up
- ✧ Patience tolerates delay, trouble, upsets and survives suffering
- ✧ Dreams become reality by constant plying

Retrace your Resilience

Do you shy from challenges? Have you an acceptable limit before you finally give up? Does discouragement numb your nerves into inactivity? Do you dwell in the pity and shame after a failed attempt?

Resilience is making a choice to get back into contention after a clumsy start. It is the 'never say die' attitude manifested in the face of failure. It is the courage to proceed in spite of obvious impediments. It is the resurrection power sustained by comeback inertia. The characteristic of resilience is an elasticity seen in no other, but the stretched spring.

Resilience is the means to reform in spite of deformation. 'Once bitten, twice shy' is your daily adage, and needless to say, it speaks volumes. It carries greater premium to be twice cautious than twice shy when tackling challenges. It would be a greater tragedy to shy off after a fall.

A dose of courage with a little caution is just sufficient to safeguard against flipping off. Being wide eyed on ventures is better, far better than locking the door and ducking behind the temporary fort of allure and comfort.

True character of resilience demands that the individual shakes off the dust to set out over again. Fourth year on campus was my typical case in point, an opportunity which allowed me to test this talisman called resilience. The recovery from a rare blow in the then concluded exams inspired little courage in me. It came nevertheless as a choice moment to redeem my battered 'role icon' image and most importantly earn me a slot in final year.

This year was critical to my expectations, and had to honor its billing as a brazen contest pitting resolve against hopelessness.

You certainly agree that juggling isn't a mere walk in the park. Not when stakes are at optimum! Such an act would be seen as an art in futility. Obvious odds notwithstanding, keep juggling patiently and carefully. Juggling may not always result in biting the dust.

Imagine for a moment; General Secretary- Main Campus Christian Union, Student representative- Board of Directors at Ufungamano House, Treasurer – University of Nairobi Christian Unions among other responsibilities. It was for these reasons difficult to swallow another pill of failure.

College precincts were always abuzz with programmes. Endless activism and zero serenity was mostly the case. Throngs of yahoos did not cease their persistent occupation of campus grounds. Having organized marches on and off campus before gave me the rare chance of ubiquity. It was payback time! Yes, for the many occasions I had booked my name in the annals of influence.

Reviewing my dozen 'fifteen minutes' of fame, when my networks with the lofty saw me interact closely with leading lights such as Kenya's then vice-president, Kalonzo Musyoka, former anti-corruption Czar and influential speaker, Professor P.L.O Lumumba among other luminaries exerted pressure on me to stretch beyond mediocre.

I had failed in the previous year! This was a different year now, and a different ball game altogether. Most importantly, performance was needed to back my enviable credentials. Fearing for the worst, I contemplated withdrawal, a plight shared by close friends. With the withdrawal draft carefully worded and conviction at optimum, it only but took resilience to keep the letter from the chairman of the Electrical Engineering department.

Resilience was the incubator that yielded the ideal conditions necessary for maturation. The choice of sitting the exams was not the difficult one, but how to ruin the ghosts through my 'version of resilience'.

The seed of resilience is found in courage. It is the magic wand that sustains the rebound-ability in our endeavors.

'I learned that courage was not the absence of fear,' said the South African freedom Icon, Nelson Mandela 'but the triumph over it. The brave man is not he who does not feel afraid, but he who conquers that fear.'

REMEMBER

- ⊕ Resilience is making a choice to get back into contention after a clumsy start
- ⊕ Resilience is the means to reform in spite of deformation
- ⊕ Greater tragedy is in shying off after a fall
- ⊕ Being wide eyed is better, far better than locking the door
- ⊕ Juggling may not always result in biting the dust
- ⊕ Resilience incubates the necessary conditions for dream maturation
- ⊕ The seed of resilience is found in courage

Take the journey called Change

The day was Tuesday, July 2, 2013 and I had just booked myself into Kenyatta National Hospital for check-up, not so regular. The weekend had been really long, going by how early in the week I had chosen to visit hospital.

After ordering some random tests, the doctor gazed at me and sought for my medical history, and my parent's. Taking his stethoscope, he probed my chest and promptly asked for my diet, typically.

The blood pressure was elevated and the red flags pointed to my diet. 160/ 105 for blood pressure is a reading unusually high, and might have just been the main cause for the awful headache I suffered.

'Patrick, we shall put you on some pressure tablets,' said the doctor with a genuine look of concern. 'Your pressure is bad', he added. 'What's the cause doc?' I promptly inquired. 'Lifestyle.', he proffered without hesitation.

Our conversation picked steam, exploring the dangers of excess table salt, sugar, red meat and many other foods in a typical dietary composition. He further emphasized the benefits of having a regular exercise routine and a healthy diet.

As he wound up, I pressed him for whatever alternatives there was to taking medication. Yes! Your guess is just as right- a lifestyle change and I took it. I promised to back up my intentions with genuine action. Actions- they say, speak louder than empty words!

I did not fancy drugs as a favorable restorative to my apparent lifestyle condition. On the contrary, I lobbied for a lifestyle overhaul. Like I told the doctor, so should you be able to reaffirm- keep the medicines out of reach for as long as you can streamline your crippling lifestyle.

It has been routinely demonstrated how by our sharp teeth we keep digging up our graves each day. Genuine change is backed by strong convictions. Embracing change means one thing- making the U-turn and heading in the opposite direction.

My lifestyle change saved me the medical bills that were sure to follow had I not made a genuine turnaround.

Instead of just sitting and bemoaning your present ordeal, get up and formulate your preliminary policy change. Write and closely monitor your new lifestyle routine. Get up early for the day. Quite frankly, you can never act the same way and expect different results.

It is that genuine change that begets a desired outcome. Some amount of change is honestly needed. A change of habits, friends, job, association and most crucial- mind set.

Some of those rabid habits need to be quickly overhauled. Remember, habits die hard and their continual entertainment portends obvious dangers. Some of these habits have no beneficial attachments to them apart from the precious time they rob us.

These noxious habits if unchecked may hamper our resourcefulness, cause impairment of vision and net gains reversal.

REMEMBER

- To back up your intentions with genuine action
- To succeed, you've got to streamline your crippling lifestyle
- Genuine change is only backed by strong convictions
- To write down and closely monitor your new lifestyle
- You can never act the same way and expect different results
- To make your change of; Habits, friends, job, association and most crucial-Mind set

CHAPTER 2

Work Your Way Up! - It Must Break Some Sweat

> "Whatsoever your hand finds to do, do
> it with your might; for there is no work,
> nor device, nor knowledge, nor wisdom,
> in the grave, where you go."
>
> (Ecc 9:10 KJV 2000)

Success does not come on a silver platter. If it did, it certainly missed course and is plotting an imminent exit. So get tasked!

There are topics that can be taught quite easily without rubbing the audiences the wrong way -and I dare say, work and its ethics is not one of these topics. Work is in the short list of subjects whose enrollment is really low.

Just like childbirth, every woman adores their bundle of joy, but I'm yet to see any that craves the labor room. The fruits are always welcome any day, save for the means.

There are those by whose refer to work as a curse. I stand to be corrected, yet however, reading Genesis chapter 3:19 and its reference to sweat of the brow does not sound to me like a curse. In fact, it avers a curse for the ground and exhorts mankind to work.

While attending one of my regular sessions in a gym at the heart of Nairobi, I took notice of one particular feature of the regular goers. In spite of the weight suspended on the barbell, there was always a constant effort to press the weight. At one corner of the room, a poster carried the words, 'No pain, No Gain!' and further across, 'No sweat, No Muscle!' And much yonder, from where I stood, imposing images of world famed bodybuilders displayed on the gym wall.

Most resplendent was not the weights that hung from the barbells. Neither did any importance issue from the posters that spoke volumes. What I found fascinating was the level of strain, sweat and dexterity at the centre of the gym.

Particularly interesting were the strange sounds let out with each thrust of the weight and the mirrors faithfully reported back every iota of muscle built and toned.

One stinging paragraph on work is a popular Bible verse, "I went by the field of the slothful and by the vineyard of the man void of understanding; And, lo, it was all grown over with thorns, and weeds had covered its face, and its stone wall was broken down. Then I saw, and considered it well: I looked upon it, and received instruction. Yet a little sleep, a little slumber, a little folding of the hands to sleep: So shall your poverty come like a robber; and your want like an armed man." (Pro 24: 30-34 KJV 2000)

In one of his teaching series, Bishop David Oyedepo, quotes Thomas A. Edison, and draws semblance existing between opportunity to a man dressed in overalls. According Oyedepo, opportunity is often missed by most people because it dresses in overalls and resembles work. And quite naturally, overalls are indicative of work. As such, not many will give thought to opportunity under such a guise. Work must nevertheless be embraced as a critical component for nurturing success.

The highway to success is one littered with numerous turns and bends. One fact is however clear- work is an indispensable function of that journey that leads to the Treasure Island.

Burning the midnight oil has to cease as a mere idiomatic expression intended for linguistic jingoism. The midnight oil must be fully utilized as a way of coinciding potential with endeavor.

Within each of us lie a potential that we are yet to fully summon. We are literally making use of only a small part of these resources. Take a peek at what Professor William James said, 'Compared to what we ought to be, we are only half awake. We are making use of only a small part of our physical and mental resources. Stating the thing broadly, the human individual thus lives far within his limits. He possesses powers of various sorts which he habitually fails to use'

It is a common charge to make hay when the sun shines. Much better still is to make hay and wait for the sun to shine on it. Opportunities are certain to come in different sizes and shapes. Not all of them come red-hot. Some will knock feebly and just once whereas others may knock at your neighbor's door.

Waiting for opportunity to knock at your door is the height of futility. Throw open your door instead, and seek for that desired opportunity. Work for it and it will not disappoint.

REMEMBER

- ⊕ Success does not come on a silver platter
- ⊕ Genius is one percent inspiration and ninety-nine percent perspiration

- No pain, No gain
- Work is a critical component for nurturing success
- The highway to success is littered with numerous turns and bends
- It is at the coincidence of potential and endeavor that success is birthed
- To make hay and wait for the sun to shine

Dedication makes all the difference

I do not quite possess the undisputed status of hard work per-se. But one classic example that invigorates my memory is the enduring spirit of hard work as was demonstrated by my own mother. Growing up in the idyllic shores of Lake Victoria, Kisumu town of western Kenya offered an exploration opportunity for our young minds.

Having been transferred into the town, she was stationed at New Nyanza general hospital as a registered nurse. I guess money was hard to come by and opulence a far cry. That financial strain was not in doubt. My father had just begun work at his new station of Kenya Commercial Bank in Taita- Taveta, Kenya.

Hard as I have previously tried, I have never quite fathomed how mama managed to work round the clock, doing day and night shifts. Just recently, I got her to reminisce about this energy- sapping routine that became her norm in the early nineties.

Mama's day didn't begin normally as yours would ordinarily. It is unclear whether it began at the wee hours of dawn or at dusk. What stood out was her attendance to patients at New Nyanza General hospital for the day followed by a brief stint attending to our obvious needs before finally departing for the night shift at Lake nursing home.

Mama's hodgepodge of home-baked buns and cookies that she sold to patients and their minders remained closely by her side. At the weekend, she promptly hired out space at the municipal market to retail clothes, agricultural produce and other merchandise.

How she managed with minimal sleep hours has to this date baffled me. Cutely remarkable is that we lacked nothing. My mom's dedication only proved that perspiration is indispensible in the quest for success.

Establish your benchmark

Too much ambition they say maketh a frustrated man. Too little, gets him nowhere. A benchmark is a standard, made with one goal – To stretch the innate ability. There is always an intrinsic quality lying in each of us that can only be roused by a raised bar.

A benchmark is a reference point whereupon an individual may compare his or her performance against best in class. Benchmarking serves to measure performance using agreeable indicators.

It is difficult to attain anything outside your line of sight. Benchmarks are designed to graduate you from one level lower to the next level higher, as ability enlarges.

Weaning is one classic example of how benchmarks are set. At the outset, it is pretty obvious that milk comprises a lion share of the infants' diet. With time though, a benchmark is set for the infants. This is critical the moment when babies get accustomed to solid food.

Benchmarks in our lives are comparable to weaning programs. In these scenarios however, objectives are set and sights trained on them to realize them. These objectives are the bench marks that every pursuer of success must establish. In other words, every person should establish benchmarks to give them something against which to press.

Quite frankly, life will throw anything at you if you have no choice.

REMEMBER

- ✦ There is an intrinsic quality lying in each of us
- ✦ It is difficult to attain anything outside your line of sight
- ✦ To realize objectives, you must train sights on them
- ✦ Without a choice, life will throw anything at you

Turn your ignition

Have you ever stopped to imagine the power of the ignition switch in a locomotive, or imagined the force behind it? If you haven't, it would be difficult to understand the logic of sparking potential. Engines are designed to scale up energy from near negligible to point of constant motion. It is all in getting fired up!

Most fires need nothing, but a little sparking to raze an entire forest. Great engines need but a simple ignition. The struggles notwithstanding, get your ignition key switch. It will get you to your destination. You don't have to tow or push your way through. Not at the expense of an ignition switch. When you locate the spark, you are home and dry.

Most folks are reclined in the cabins of their struggles and hopelessly wondering how to traverse their vast worlds. The proximity between our ruts and desired destinations is an ignition away. Like bulldozers, every person has an in-borne potential of creating a beaten path with which to access their destinations.

Be not dismayed, neither be you alarmed by your present struggle, for it is just as important to you as is in finding your ignition switch. That which is often referred to as a spark of genius is the ignition key, the very outstanding key you've got to look out for.

We've got great engines deep down; great forests- forests that make the Amazon seem mere shrubs. What we very much need is a simple ignition, a spark to set the embers ablaze.

REMEMBER

- When you locate your spark, you're virtually home and dry
- The proximity between our ruts and desired destinations is an ignition away

Begin early, begin little, rest a little later

> "And on the seventh day God ended his
> work which he had made; and he rested
> on the seventh day from all his work
> which he had made."
>
> (Genesis 2:2 KJV 2000)

There is no better way to fight procrastination than by holding out little by little, and taking the deserved rest a little later. This is the genius of the diminutive ant and the brilliance of the honey bee. The proper way to deal with our assignments is to fill up the minute we're in, captured in the magic of taking one step at a time.

The creator is a classic example of how work and rest should be sequenced. Rest must come after work, not the other way round. Rest should be earned, paid by the currency called work. There is no greater tragedy than resting and yawning in the morning with a hope of working a little later. This warped ideology accounts for one of the greatest undoing in the developing world.

After God had determined the creation work available for Him to accomplish, He apportioned each day a sizeable amount of work. At the close of each day, He reckoned that all the day's work was done and that it was perfect.

31

How often do you postpone your assignments and duties? Do you prefer to carry forward your tasks in the hope of sorting them out later? Is your later better than never? Do you habitually put off meetings to a further notice? Do you re-adjust your wake-up alarm to grab more slumber? If your answers are yes to these, then you are just another procrastinator.

Each day demands its own share of tasks that must be dispensed with and shoved aside. A postponement routine triggers the unfortunate habit of piling up. Such a routine creates a backlog which eventually cripples our endeavors.

Procrastination is the 'I will do it later' attitude. It is the 'better late than never' culture. It is a way of pacifying the will, and does well to establish a kind of comfort that assumes that later is just as good, as long as the assignment is finally executed.

In the struggle against failure, it is foremost to vanquish the thought of 'better late than never'. Each time we face up to a new challenge, we've got to realize that we are a day older than when we fell asleep. Time doesn't wait for us to align our programmes.

There's always a false allure associated with a little rest and slumber. However, the moment you postpone an urgent mission and prop your weight on a couch, then you must be able to answer a few stubborn questions. First, did you schedule time for a little slumber in the programme? Second, will the assignment be waived by the mere act of postponement? Third, does a little slumber guarantee a restful mind at last?

A little slumber never guarantees rest to the mind at all. In fact, there is always a persistent discomfort creeping in the hindsight which keeps the mind rattled with any pending work.

It is not difficult to tell whether or not you are a procrastinator. The signs are always evidenced by our mobilization and utilization of the resource called time.

One derailing attitude set up by procrastination is discouragement. It is when utensils heap up in the kitchen sink that discouragement sets in, and the resulting reek easily repels the positive will to clean up. When you accumulate substantial dust atop the cabinet, any dusting attempts are spontaneously thwarted by the constant sneezing resulting in unnecessary delays.

To live is privilege, to die is duty. And nobody is ever prepared to leave the scene. The Biblical King Hezekiah in second Kings 20, sought more time to accomplish his pending projects. Death lurks in the corner and comes moments before you're ready for it.

We are actually closer to our exits than the last time we retired to bed. Death has perfected the art of stealth in more than a thousand ways. And so while we live, we must utilize our time really well, for we'll be gone, maybe sooner than we actually thought.

Before long, age also catches up with our plans and weakens both sinew and resolve. Soon after, we begin to transfer our vision to the next generation, and for the majority who do not pass the baton, their graves fill up with unexploited talent. This is often due to failure to execute blueprints before taking the journey for eternity.

Slow and steady wins the race. Without steady, slow loses it's grip of the statement, and the luster of this proposition dies. It is worthwhile to value the opportunities that come our way daily.

REMEMBER

- To fight procrastination, hold out little by little
- Rest must be earned, paid upfront by the currency called work

- Each day demands its own share of tasks that must be dispensed with and shoved aside
- Time doesn't wait for any of us to align our individual plans
- Slow and steady wins the race

Polish up!

There is only one way to acquiring sheen, and it's all in building a rich knowledge base. The acquisition of knowledge remains the surest way to increasing likeability and appeal. Brilliance, otherwise known as sheen is the ability to reflect brightness and by it illuminating the surrounding.

Knowledge is power, and the individual who bears it gets along easily. I have come to appreciate the magic of the words, 'Knowledge is power.' These words emblazoned my elementary school badge for years on end. I've come to appreciate these days that the more you become knowledgeable, the more mature you become. It is not age that matures a person, but information.

We live in a tumultuous world where ignorance has become astronomical. Most of the global mess today is traceable to a general lack of knowledge. It is particularly succinct that people perish for lack of this asset whose poverty has no defense.

In court rooms today, not even a choreographed feigning of ignorance will earn you a lenient charge. In other words, knowledge is an insurance against unforeseen perils coming your way. It is the same knowledge that elevates you to a pedestal and sets you apart as truly distinguished.

Whether you live in the developed or developing world, there is always a renewed push to acquire new knowledge. This acquisition would easily narrow to the colossal disparities that exist between the knowledgeable and ignorant.

The world we live in is stuck in some kind of darkness and requires intense illumination. The bearer of light often leads the way, otherwise the entire troupe lands in the ditch. 'Knowledge is Light', the ever-so-dominant motto which schools emblazoned on their emblems remains the one slogan that has persistently guided school folks to this day and age.

The sustained acquisition of knowledge liberates from the dark cellars of ignorance. Today, job interviews and examinations test for knowledge, among several other parameters. Therefore, apart from self confidence, presentation skills and experience, the knowledge borne and relevant application is also tested.

A sustained reading culture not only makes a person more relevant but also increases his confidence levels.

REMEMBER

- ⊕ The acquisition of knowledge remains the surest way to increasing likeability and appeal
- ⊕ Knowledge is an insurance is an insurance against unforeseen perils
- ⊕ The bearer of light often leads the way
- ⊕ A reading culture often increases a persons confidence levels

CHAPTER 3

Get Your Cake Right

The statement 'If you won't get it right, don't do it just yet' doesn't inspire much confidence. It nonetheless bears some moral bearing.

But, wait a minute!

Have you ever sunk your teeth on half-baked cakes? I'm certain they don't taste nice. 'Hot cakes' might be the single 'hottest' bites in town, save for the quality of the cakes. In the true sense of the word, you don't have to bake cakes; you've got to bake them just right.

Time is critical to any activity, and good cakes don't fly off the oven. No, they are worth the duration they take in the oven.

Occasionally, our systems churn out half-baked cakes- fast enough to reduce production costs. When this happens, quality becomes compromised and hence the global mess we see today. Truth is; the present cases of confusion are the consequences of hurried programmes!

It doesn't pay to rush vital processes. In fact, over speeding does cause fatalities and our highways clearly attest to that perfectly well. Speed is of essence, but against quality, we've got to strike the right balance. On a more critical activity, do not hesitate to give speed the back seat!

My math experience finds relevance here. On the several occasions when I managed thirty-or-so percentage points after a gruesome two-and-a-half hour toil, I pretty much understood that the score should have been equivalent to five or six questions correctly answered. Strangely, my exam booklet was normally filled-up with workings, and no substantial score to prove for the toil.

My biggest undoing was the same thought that the faster I filled my exam booklet, the better chance I had to score high marks. But alas! To my horror, the result never changed. Not once. It was still in the neighborhood of thirties and ranked me somewhere at bottom of class. What you'd call a typical case of doing things in the same manner and expecting different results.

With time however, I gathered the confidence to evenly distribute the allocated hundred and fifty minutes to a set of six questions carefully identified. I soon realized that each of these sums took up twenty five minutes. What economic waste! That was the deepest conviction which pushed me to devise an economic plan for the hundred and fifty minutes. What I called the 'ten-minutes-each' plan.

This new plot saw each question allocated a working duration of ten minutes irrespective of how menial it appeared. Any extra minutes was spent on re-checking the working to make sure no error sneaked undetected. The trick worked perfectly and the fifteen time-capsules were just sufficient to solve fifteen sums accurately. This time though, my pace was controlled by the forced pace control edict. A few weeks later, I was honored with my first ever gift for a stellar performance in Math.

The moment my name was called out among the top scorers of the contest, not a few eyebrows rose and my booklet was withdrawn for further scrutiny. My response was swift- 'I've got the secret to cracking the spine of Math, and I will fail it no more.' And true to my word, I churned straight A's all the way to the national examinations. What a turnaround!

I hold dearest the urgency of the moment folks, but against quality, make the time you spend on your project really count.

REMEMBER

- A good cake is worth the duration it takes in an oven
- Against quality, the time spent on a project should count for much more

Chisel the correct grooves

Every lock has a unique key. So, whether you brandish a diamond or platinum key is both cosmetic and immaterial. For any key, the rule of thumb is to have the right groove chiseled on it. The number of keys in your bunch also means nothing and more so if the right key pattern be missing.

In view of this, carving of the perfect key-groove becomes the greatest concern. The development process of development is a gradual metamorphosis, akin to beveling a persona which fits perfectly into desired design.

Every key must possess a unique 'key configuration', what is otherwise referred to as its DNA. Nothing else unlatches the lock.

In life, 'right grooves' is a debatable topic observable from several perspectives. I can not enlist these at all. One thing is however true- that is; these grooves have the effect of making a person likable and contagious. It has to do with those personality issues that endear you to the people around you. It is those little features which make your presence enjoyable and your association a moment to behold.

The right papers alone or even experience may not open our doors as these alone have little sway. Cutting the right groove however carries much sway.

I do not wish to belabor here, but among your vital grooves are; a firm handshake, that honest smile, an upright gait, a friendly language, a strong and controlled voice, a tidy outlook and very crucial- an ability to listen.

These are the things we've got to take up and get locks easing on our advances.

REMEMBER

- ⊕ Every lock has its unique key
- ⊕ Cutting the right groove carried much sway

Let the dots wait

In his short narration, 'Uncle Ben's choice', Chinua Achebe advances the need for caution ahead of every decision. Uncle Ben is caught between two worlds, with the winds of civilization fast and sweeping. One thing is very apparent- Uncle Ben's reminiscence of his grandpa's caution to confine handshakes below the elbow.

Apart from handshakes, Uncle Ben was admonished against sleeping with both eyes closed. Any thoughtful son of Africa was not to take anything for chance. Choices in his perspective had grave consequences and decisions had to be thought over, literally.

When the deal gets too good, think again, so the saying goes. However, with devils in the details, caution is often overlooked and decisions fly without careful prognosis.

Honestly, where is the point of hurrying decisions when the outcome might be regrettable? Careful consideration ahead of decisions is the best foot forward. Informed decisions are normally instrumental to success. Taking decisions pronto is just fine. However, thoughtfulness pronto is instrumental too to making desired outcomes.

On the verge of decisions, make sure to find real value in tying the dots before scribbling on the blanks. Take care to avoid the mad rush of appending signatures before referring to the annexed documents.

Regulations, instructions and terms form part and parcel of our daily undertaking and commitments. Some are wordy and often lengthy, and require clear understanding. Yet, despite these far-reaching implications, not much thought is allowed to caution.

Examination regulations, legal papers, medical procedures, business contracts and many other documents require careful consideration before our commitment is given.

Success rests upon the foundation of proper and firm decision. A careful balancing act enables the devils in the details to be completely exorcised.

It is more propitious to delay weighty decisions rather than rue the loss of opportunity as a result of inappropriate action. Always find time to think over matters before their execution. It is by such means that you may intuitively know where your paces might get you.

Before you sign that hot deal, or make a vow. Before you o.k. your next offer or sign the humongous transfer, it is just the right thing to let the dots wait; Yes, to wait for as long as it takes to tie them up.

REMEMBER

- The choices we make often have far-reaching consequences
- Informed decisions are normally instrumental to success
- Success rests upon the foundation of proper and firm decisions
- The dots should wait, yes! For as long as it takes to tie them up

CHAPTER 4

Establish the Right Focus

"To distract is to destruct"

The lens is not your ordinary glass. It is a kind of glass with an ability of focus. It concentrates energy both light and heat to a focal centre. This is the genius of focus.

The moment you project rays onto a lens, it reciprocates by concentrating those same rays to a focal point resulting in intense energy and may sometimes result in a fire. Try the same on a piece of paper and notice the imminence of focus. The sun is a great source of energy. However, it is not until we employ the genius of focus that its rays may be stepped up into substantive energy for greater impact.

There are occasions when success demands nothing but focus. It is that critical ability to remain engrossed on the assignment at hand with an aim of releasing unprecedented outcomes.

Typical molecular motion results in a multidirectional movement and an imminent loss of energy. The only means to generate inertia and confront the challenge of the moment is to concentrate on that which is billed as critical.

Undivided attention yields stellar performance and produces stars! It is upon the lynchpin of focus that every thunderbolt firms up its hold.

The greatest solvent of quality is distraction. That the division of focus is the premier cause of distraction is no hidden secret. Whenever both mental and physical capacities are confined to a point, then a clear path of goal pacification becomes visible.

Research has revealed that when oxygen is shut out of all other minor processes and concentrated to the task at hand, then the most of who we are can be easily unleashed.

The tunnels of life are unique and unprecedented. Yet each one of us has their share of tunnels to grope through. Occasionally, we'll experience darkness through our tunnels. During these moments however, we must never lose focus, lest we hit the pitfalls and drift away.

Through these forays, we must never concentrate on the din and jeers for these will certainly contribute to the constant drifting of focus. It is important to manage the journey and hold to modicum and peace.

The world today has several focus drifters; So much more than in all the previous generations combined. It has become more difficult than ever before to keep the mind focused.

These drifters, I beg your pardon include the century old television and radio. It isn't surprising that these gadgets have invaded our lives so much so that no room in our homes has been spared their reach.

The modern family has today admitted the television set into every corner of their homes. In my routine electrical services design, majority of clients have often insisted that television outlets be provided in every room- bedroom, lounges, dining and other non conventional areas.

As the information age asserts its boisterous influence; several folks are always eager to keep their tech-savvy egos keen. Distraction has become handier today than ever before. We've got an entire generation tugging iPods, talking over Skype and possibly downloading videos on the tube. Most houses today are perky for days on end. Presently, silence has become a foreign word in most homes.

The lifeblood of focus is concentration and a call to focus is a subtle call to practice concentration. Life in Africa offers the continent a rare opportunity to appreciate the African eagle and its superior record in preying. The eagle hones its ability to concentrate from a tender age.

When aiming for a kill, the eagle must train their sights on prey several yards below. Despite the open skies, an eagle has an amazing success rate with every hunt. It is therefore not surprising that an eagle can focus on its target from a mile away.

Apart from great vision, probably five times better than the human eye, the eagle successfully conceals her shadow from prey. These skills make the eagle dominant in the soaring heights.

Like the mother-eagle, parents must coach their own children on the life lessons of concentration. Loss or lack of concentration is traceable to restlessness and impatience-obvious signs of fading attention.

Parents and other guardians must take in some vital lessons. Firstly, there has to be a particular family hour, at which time every electronic gadget is to be turned off. Above all, every parent must take full control of entertainment in their own houses.

Unfortunately for many, most houses have found in the last born kid the undisputed deejay, taking entertainment to the next level. These kids superintend over the remote control from the early cartoon days through to teenage years, and do not make matters any better for the family unit. In fact, it is a habit that corrupts the family order and sponsors untold chaos.

Best practice would require incorporation of programmes in our schools' syllabi to help students regain their waning concentration. This should be every parent's investment.

REMEMBER

- Success demands focus
- Undivided attention yields stellar performance and produces stars
- The greatest solvent of quality is distraction
- The lifeblood of focus is in concentration

Sober up!

Don't drink and drive! If you must, take water for your journey. These are some popular caution signs that find relevance along highways and road stretches in the countryside. Still others find their space in the jammed city streets. Consumption of alcohol in excess is perilous! This is another hazard sign associated with intoxication.

There's great need for sobriety in the journeys we take. Further afield, enforcement authorities have their mandate cut out to apprehend individuals who attempt to juggle the bottle and the wheel. In the journey of life, everyone is a driver-and none holder of a licence, valid or otherwise.

We live in a society where sobriety counts in every way. It is a new dawn in our world, where a carefree and wanton razzmatazz may easily be cause for your trouble. The journey of life needs a dispassionate, steady and a rational mind. Like all other journeys, life needs a watchful hand to navigate it.

My discourse on sobriety shouldn't suggest that a mere avoidance of alcohol may guarantee soundness. Not at all! Sobriety is evidenced by the quality of judgments we make, intoxicated or not. It is the ability to execute a thoughtful consideration ahead of every decision. Sobriety is the capacity to conjure sound and sensible judgment at the point of decision.

Everyone makes regrettable choices and costly mistakes. This is demonstrated by how casual we sometimes get with life. All of us have appalling moments. On a fast lane however, critical decisions must come in handy before your next turn, lest you overshoot your bends.

Sobriety is an outcome of a clear mindset, free of erratic manipulations. Utmost concentration is foremost when getting things together.

Research has proven that alcoholic content has capacity to alter the thought process and affect reason. Essentially, intoxication has the effect of portraying things somehow different from what they appear in reality. It may portray surfaces as skewed and disarrayed.

Ahead of crucial decisions, individuals may be advised to limit intoxication as a means to balanced thinking and a requirement for sound decisions.

REMEMBER

- ✦ In the journey of life, everyone is a driver-and none holder of a licence
- ✦ The journey of life needs a dispassionate, steady and rational mind
- ✦ Sobriety is measured by the quality of judgments we make

- Everyone makes regrettable choices and costly mistakes
- Sobriety is an outcome of a clear mindset, free of erratic manipulations

Sacrifice- It's the single most valued investment

Have you ever turned off your most cherished television programme, - to get an assignment out of the way? How about trading your entertainment for duty? That is the essence of sacrifice. Sacrifice is an investment whose earnings are certain to materialize.

It is getting involved with an undertaking, not because of its face value but due to its ultimate reward. At times, you've got to make clear item lists of the sacrifices you intend to make. Without these, no sacrifices may ever be made. And make no mistake about this- the cheque called sacrifice pays at maturity- not earlier. It does pay in the long run, not in the short term.

Growing up, I picked a knack for crossword puzzles. With time, scrabble joined the fray. It soon became apparent that both codeword and crossword puzzles were getting the better of me. To whet my appetite for these, I made it my commitment to secure the dailies for the purpose of solving the puzzles therein.

Just before campus, a job at a local Secondary School became my answered prayer and as fate would have it, the staff newspaper became my optimal attraction. I didn't quite notice how much it strained my relationship with colleagues and significantly distracted me from core business- teaching.

Habits die hard; you well fathom. When university came knocking, so with me travelled the hobby-in-chief-crossword puzzle! Like other recreational pastimes, it afforded a feeling of actualization. And I must admit it, I still take these puzzles in my stride, albeit occasionally.

The puzzles are still heart and center in their entertainment capacities and in their offer of mental challenge. It is however important to strike a balance of time resource in view of the bigger picture lest focus be completely lost.

University of Nairobi's Jomo Kenyatta Memorial Library offered me a brilliant spot for my choicest sport. My first stop in the library was at the newspaper section, at which point I conveniently pulled out the newspaper leaves I saw relevant. Unlike soccer or rugby whose umpires are always at hand to officiate the game, I had myself both to play and umpire on my own terms.

Before long, I became guilty of violating my own terms by exceeding the time limits I had set. Worse still, I couldn't restrict myself to the daily puzzles alone, but instead foraged into the archives for even greater challenges.

Crisis set in when I started gathering newspapers as old as the university itself. The archived newspapers were securely bound- and handier to deal with. I can recollect that some had the Royal College of East Africa stamp on them- That's how deep into the archives I descended.

Such was a juvenile duty; futile even with my lopsided self appraisal. Study time grew shorter on the occasions I got puzzled ahead of studying. On one such occasion I remember, no sooner had I just settled to begin studying than the evacuation siren blared on my dull ears.

How I wished things were different the moment I saw students checking out of the library having accomplished something really worthwhile. On this particular occasion, I was left with one lonely horse to ride on – and you guessed it just right, a hearty wish! The last straw was a rock solid commitment to take measured steps toward redemption.

Eventually, I traded entertainment for business, puzzle for study and graduation the bigger picture.

There are similar priorities- misplaced as ever, which call for a complete makeover for dreams to materialize. Success is only a sacrifice away. Remember, it is only through faithful regulation that success may result. So, keep the thrills away! Yes, for as long as time will afford them later for your delight.

These days, whenever Premier league fever nudges me in that familiar way, I can't help but resist the urge of becoming my hapless former shell. I occasionally struggle with these battles, even though a lot has since changed.

Successful people make sizeable sacrifices as sure means to securing their most cherished goals. Why should it be very difficult to keep away our distractions for a little while, even as we hold dear our individual pursuits? This is the meaning of sacrifice.

REMEMBER

- ⊕ Sacrifice is an investment whose earnings are certain to materialize
- ⊕ The cheque called sacrifice pays at maturity- Not earlier

- ⊕ Above all else, it is much more critical to strike a balance of time
- ⊕ Success is often a sacrifice away
- ⊕ Successful people make sizeable sacrifices as sure means to securing cherished goals

CHAPTER 5

Hercules was Created

> "Ask, and it shall be given you; seek, and you shall find; knock, and it shall be opened unto you: For every one that asks receives; and he that seeks finds; and to him that knocks it shall be opened."
>
> (Matthew 7:7-8 KJV 2000)

Hercules, painted as a valiant hero in Greek mythology is an iconic symbol of endowment. What is doubtful is whether nature may richly endow a single individual with attributes which make dependability count for nothing. It is needless to toil independently when help is within reach. Without the much needed help, the waters we navigate might overwhelm us.

Several people endure failure and struggle with a hope of stumbling upon success some day. Many more barely scrape through their sore, protracted struggles. At the end of the tunnel, a survival is earned, but little to show for their punishing ordeals. The most incredible reality is that these struggles are often borne in loneliness. Sufferers prefer to isolate themselves. The argument, after all, the privileged also withdraw to their high ends, among their ilk.

The most disturbing trend is that across the agony of suffering, folks do so with grave secrecy and 'carry own crosses' with a degree of guarded confidentially, as though suffering independently lessens the pain.

The struggles of life have consistently alienated people and set them on a path of solitude. Suffering feels detaching and shameful no doubt. However, the more a crisis is shared the lighter its burden becomes.

That notion that image gets soiled with every appeal for help is misleading. No man is an island to exist on their own. An appeal for help only shows how dependable you really are.

Unfortunately, many have yielded their precious time and energies to be battered by the blizzard of failure. Resources are sapped by an adamant refusal to admit weakness and the need of help.

'Any fool can try to defend his mistakes,' said Carnegie, '-and most fools do – but it raises one above the herd and gives one a feeling of nobility and exultation to admit one's mistakes.'

It's almost genetic to project an image of invincibility, even in difficulty. It is very this egocentric human nature that insists on minding one's business even when tides are low. Species; terrestrial, aquatic or even arboreal wouldn't expose the underbelly of weakness lest it be exploited by competitors.

Reality is, sticking to the gun at whatever cost and a continued refusal to accept alternative opinion is a perfect precipitate for failure. What it does best- quick decimation!

It takes great courage to admit difficulty. It rises above that inexcusable alternative that has always been an adamant refusal to concede. No retreat- no surrender remains a philosophy that everyone should subscribe to. However, seeking help is not an admission of surrender neither is it a retreat. No. It is an injection of stimulus and a boost to ability. An admission of defeat is also a positive step because it allows you to clearly see an alternative persuasion. So, be it in politics, business or in educational circles, it profits a lot to admit weakness followed by an invitation for help.

Like in sports, the pursuit of success requires the input of others to both grow and glow. Every goal is usually a net effect of taps from other members of the team. The life we live is not a-hundred-meters dash. It is a marathon, and Paul Tergat knows that forty-two kilometers is best conquered in the company of your training colleagues. There is only one sure dwelling for psyche- Company!

In the right direction, a considerable amount of support is indeed required. In our world of diminishing resources, you may never get assistance until you admit vulnerability and lethargy. After all, help is not inexhaustible resource to lie idle.

I have all the more appreciated the value of support from my short gym stint. In the gym, some weights can never be lifted without support. During gym sessions, trained instructors are always at hand to offer guidance as and when needed.

Every so often, you will hear calls for support from pockets of weightlifters across the gymnasium, at which point help is conveniently given.

One particular incident came when the gym instructor leaned over to buttress the back of a weight-carrying lifter. The instructor's arms wrapped around the lifter's torso and palms firmed against the ribcage. At which point, both individuals descended with the humongous weights, resting on a bar and pressing against the lifter's shoulder.

What a selfless way to support another! There are things we'll never accomplish without support and those that we may never perfect minus support. Everyone needs an amount of support to go over their most improbable mountains.

Whenever challenges come, you must count for the experience and expertise of those who have journeyed the route before. In the true sense of the word, pioneers are nonexistent; every so called, has more or less had the privilege of stepping on the shoulders of those that went ahead of him.

Since all of us have their areas of expertise, it should be normal to let others guide us through the avenues where our navigation would appear bothersome. In the end, what others have through ingenuity, we've got a chance of acquiring by a balanced combination of training, experience and most crucial-help.

Just after graduation, I turned to gym and swimming, but more especially to swimming. Swimming was especially fun in the September sun. It was recreational no doubt, yet also occupied the time slots that came with the cessation of lectures.

Having missed out on swimming experience early in life, I wasn't going to let this golden chance elude me. The pool, conveniently located in a neighbouring estate attracted several people including kids.

My drills included free style, breast stroke and a bit of diving. In spite of these moves, I had not fully honed the art of inhaling air within the interval of every stroke.

So, every time I swam, I sprinted breathlessly for close to twenty meters until I crossed the entire pool width. Occasionally, I got upright quickly to replenish air when I got to the shallow end.

It was not usual to be alone at the pool. The benefits of being alone were nonetheless obvious. Firstly, the pool was spacious. Second, the water was guaranteed to remain clear for such a long time. On one such occasion, I was the only person in the pool, and superintended over by one lifeguard on duty.

A spacious pool at hand and time allowing, I earmarked every new skill to attempt. My determination was to practice how to draw in air between the strokes. Starting from the deep end, and heading for the shallow end, the momentum kicked in. Before long, I lost rhythm and started to go under.

At that point; my eyes closed, arms became clumsy and feet kicked uncontrollably. I was drowning and well conscious about it. Death was staring at me and that was certain. Every trick in my bag fell flat.

In my quick assessment, I had only one chance for a final yelp for rescue and nothing more in my ambit. With a last gasp, I thrust my head out of the water and yelled at the top of my lungs.

No sooner had I started choking than a cold steel bar pressed against my side. Heavens had clearly dispatched an angel to aid me, and one thing I vividly remember was how I lay by the pool recuperating from my initial blackout.

Thirty-First December came fast and furious. It was the last calendar date and ecstasy was priority for obvious reasons. By sunset that fateful day, the impact of my September experience came rushing back to me. It was especially harrowing to witness an unfortunate retrieval of a lifeless body from under the pool in full view of two lifeguards.

Life is a journey that requires the careful hands of a reliable life guard. You and I deserve a hand with every call for help. It's more like swimming, where a duty bound lifeguard has to be on full alert to give help as and when needed.

The Bible emphasizes the age-old formula of getting things done. "Ask, and it shall be given you; seek, and you shall find; Knock, and it shall be opened unto you: For every one that asks receives; and he that seeks finds; and to him that knocks it shall be opened" (Matthew 7:7-8 KJV 2000)

In most situations, an admission of lethargy has nothing to do with a public appeal for help. It has more to do with an acknowledgement of weakness and a genuine intention to overhaul the status quo. Instead of a hyped statement of insurrection, it will be more important to present a careful solicitation of HELP!

Sympathy is welcome, anytime. However, like empty calories, it contributes little to get you out of trouble. For the same reason, I've run into trouble with folks who insist on doling nothing but pity. Pity parties are worthless when meaningful help is available.

Sympathy is a tranquilizer that numbs the pangs of anguish. However, to shred the threads of failure, it is critical to draw the curtains on pity parties. 'Wise men never sit and wail their loss,' said Shakespeare, 'they find how to redress their harms.'

I am still convicted that a little hand here and some more there is just sufficient to pack up the momentum. Even though synergy is a great first step to gaining currency and acquiring crucial hints, outright over-reliance is detrimental to innovation. Copying destroys our innate abilities and flies in the face of our God given creativities.

There is need for diversity; for it's the only way to improve the color of life by making it more flowery and picturesque. Each of us has a couple of blank sheets on which to draft their stories as different as they come.

REMEMBER

- Without help, the waters we navigate may overwhelm us
- The more a crisis is shared, the lighter its burden becomes
- No man is an island to exist on their own
- Resources are continually sapped by an adamant refusal to admit weakness and need of help
- It takes courage to admit difficulty

- Every goal is usually a net effect of taps from other members of the team
- There is only one dwelling for psyche- It is Company!
- Life is a journey requiring the careful hands of a reliable life guard

Join a worthy coalition

"Behold, how good and how pleasant it is for brethren to dwell together in unity." (Psa 133:1)

Vision is indicative of distance, without which the people perish. This is the reason organizations draw up vision statements as a prop for their mission statements. Most of these drafts are usually a collection of each of the member's contribution.

"Two are better than one; because they have a good reward for their labor. For if they fall, the one will lift up his fellow: but woe to him that is alone when he falls; for he has not another to help him up."- (Ecclesiastes 4:9-10 KJV 2000)

I have severally considered the word 'TOGETHER', and punned with it a lot more times. Fidgeting with it flashes varied concepts to my mind, and I'm often taken aback by these. Say for instance; 'TO-GET-HER', 'TO-GET-HERE', or 'TO-GET-THERE'.

I'm sure 'to-get-there' and 'together' are more relevant to the present context. Whenever you conjure a vision, it is only obvious that your destination is a little outstretched. Your goal might be a long distance off your shore, and a formidable strategy has to be hatched to-get-there.

To get there, you need to get together, and this is the genius of involvement. We've got to put more emphasis on the worth of the coalition since not all coalitions are worth our time.

Participation is getting on board more robustly throughout the course of an activity. Practice is not participation. Whereas the former may be done in isolation, the latter requires a team spirit.

Participation provides a boost to any activity since it avails the much needed labour and a rich diversity. The moment different individuals, with varying perspectives and abilities take down a task; the outcome is an economic improvement to the time and resources pooled together.

Participation is often hinged on the strength of diversity and far reaching specialization. It is this rich diversity that makes an individual keener on a concept, yet another by routine participation acquires aptitude on the same concept. In every new challenge, remember these famous words: 'Every man I meet is my superior in some way,' as said by Emerson, 'In that, I learn of him.'

Through participation, one iron sharpens the other. It is however worrying that advocates of individualism shun participation for such reasons as; fear of being ruled irrelevant, the desire to hide perceived ignorance, the hope of avoiding criticism and the aspiration to maintain an edge over others among other convictions.

These persuasions are informed by a desire for self-preservation. So, to a greater extent, the drive for participation is always dismissed in the mad pursuit of independence. Independence is seldom achieved by working independently. Independence is a product of an assortment of individual efforts put together.

I've always had a penchant for the wild Serengeti and its Lion pride. Though the lions are not the best sprinters of all, yet they hunt down sprinters among other game. They do so by preying for game together, rallying each other to the common denominator- To bring down the hunt.

One popular Swahili saying goes **"umoja ni nguvu, utengano ni udhaifu"**, translated to mean unity natures strength, whereas disunity sponsors weakness.

To get there, how about holding together?

REMEMBER

- ⊕ Vision is indicative of distance, without which the people perish
- ⊕ Participation avails the mental boost to any activity by availing numbers
- ⊕ Participation is often hinged on the strength of diversity
- ⊕ Independence is seldom achieved by working independently
- ⊕ Whereas unity natures strength, disunity sponsors weakness

Appoint a coach

Every sportsman is always quick to acknowledge the premium of tutelage and guidance. The arena of life is no different ball game. The cares and travails of life require a formidable shoulder- a person who can get the better out of you.

A coach is a one who understands the pitfalls of the terrain either by experience or intuition, and is both willing and able to guide the way. There are many aspects to coaching that come into play. Crucial is the capacity to audit; Strength, Weaknesses, opportunities and Threats (S.W.O.T). The analysis and determination of how these attributes may be individually and collectively related with is every coach's cup of tea.

Strengths find their diametrical opposites in weaknesses, just like opportunities in threats. And like most coaches would honestly reveal, these attributes are embedded to the individuals' DNA. It is therefore futile to sweep these under the carpet. The only way out is to deal with these attributes more decisively. For instance, strength is an enabling character that makes a person effective in discharging responsibilities. On the contrary, weakness is a general display of lethargy and lack of energy.

A good coach will identify these salient attributes and design a plan to maximize strengths and stem weaknesses. The same would apply to opportunities and threats. Unlike a role model, a coach has a better opportunity to engage directly with their protégé. Due to their remote influence, a role model only has a limited chance of influencing outcomes.

REMEMBER

- ⊕ The cares and travails of life require a formidable shoulder
- ⊕ Strengths find their diametrical opposites in weaknesses, just like opportunities in threats

Survive the competition

> "If you have run with the footmen, and they have wearied you, then how can you contend with horses"
>
> (Jer 12:5 KJV 2000)

Competition is a contest for advantage that pits rivals against each other and who will spare nothing to win the contest. Rivals will do everything possible, overt or otherwise in their quest to bag top honors.

Competition was invented by Mother Nature on account of her scanty resources. Nature avails limited resources and conceals them in far off places, otherwise called treasure troves under key and lock.

Inadequacy of resources is the trigger of competition seen among plants and animals. There's always a constant angling to outwit the rest.

Competition exists everywhere. You only need to open your eyes and the next person you meet is in some kind of contest. In every corner, field or talk, there is always a tinge of competition. Moreover, automakers today spare nothing in their quest to make the fastest engines to beat the competition.

Everyone desires to get to their destinations ahead of the pack. In some exam cases, smuggling of materials into examination centers has become a big concern. Reason is to reach the destination ahead of the rest and probably without much sweat.

These overtures have pushed resources further and further away, from the access of many. Only but a few individuals use power and control to secure these resources in far off places only appropriate to their tastes and proclivity.

Adaptation thins the competition by eliminating the ill equipped and the resigned. Whereas the nimble last longer, the gauche quickly opt out of the competition. Every one has an equal chance of winning in such a race, but only with the price of dexterity paid upfront.

In the race to the top, the question is not how well rivals are prepared against to you. No, it has a lot more to do with how well you are prepared to compensate for your lack of finesse. In business, the use of advertisements to expand visibility has been deployed by all and sundry.

Several years ago while still trapped in our kiddy world, we caught a habit of playing with butterflies. As the rains eased and the drenching receded, the parched neighborhoods began to lush and the flowers blossomed like little rainbows. Curiously, at every corner where the flowers sprung up, colorful butterflies found haven.

There wasn't scarcity of games for us, but the most dominant was a prank, or so we thought that we played on the 'clueless' butterflies. With strings tied to bits of paper - cut and colored to mimic butterflies, we ran all over with butterflies hot in our trail. It mattered little the color on the paper bits, what really mattered was color- period!

Has it ever occurred to you that the probability of finding a finger print similar yours is one in close to six billion? In fact, the genetic makeup of an individual bears very remote semblance even to their identical twin. This is how expansive our universe can get, and there is no cause to feel choked by the ever growing levels of competition. Take your colored bits and get down to your trade for there are just enough butterflies in the world for every last one of us.

It is similarly important to note that our individual uniqueness offers us a more solid foundation upon which we may progress in our areas of strength.

When you get up each morning, look at your finger prints and notice their contours and patterns. In spite of the population, bursting at the seams, our genes are a definite copyright sufficient to safeguard our initiatives.

I do not disapprove the long standing philosophy of 'survival for the finest'. Survival, like taught in high school days favors the fittest. That explains why species enhance their finesse by adapting to the prevailing conditions thereby outwitting rivals.

To spice up for the competition, some creative means of enhancing finesse may come in handy. How about acquiring the best packaging for ourselves or products?

I must reiterate that packaging goes beyond mere consumables. It is vital to establish proper packaging for ourselves as means to enhancing acceptability. It would be futile to present a business proposal to a prospective investor without a proper package.

It must not escape us that a first impression bares it all. However, no longer must we hang on first impressions alone. Impressions– first or last, are impressions still and must be dangled carefully to survive the competition and earn success.

REMEMBER

- The way to get things done is to stimulate competition
- Whereas the nimble last longer, the gauche opt out of the competition
- Uniqueness offers a solid foundation upon which progress hinges
- The first impression bares it all

However hard, take initiative

> "To get through the hardest journey we need take only one step at a time, but we must keep on stepping"
>
> – Chinese proverb

There is nothing as intricate to humanity as breaking loose. Right from birth to the point of death; humanity will never paint the town red in the wake of detachment.

Even hardened inmates shed tears when breaking from incarceration to reunite with society.

The only way out of the quagmires of indecision is a bold step called detachment. With a similar conviction, build your castles in the air and when done, put foundations under them. This is the famous step called initiative- moving in the direction of the not-so-popular decision.

It takes your stepping out to realize success. There is never a perfect moment like the here and now. Yesterday is in the past, tomorrow is in the future. What we have is today. It is for that special reason that you've got to make that call now and set the appointment today.

Even though the coincidence of opportunity and preparedness sets the pace for success, it must be clarified that initiative is the sole convener of coincidence. Therefore, initiative is king.

Set the ball rolling. Break that ice. Offer that bold greeting. Through all these, you'll begin to appreciate that a journey of a thousand miles begins with one bold step- INITIATIVE.

There is a definite problem with getting easily persuaded out of your plot, more so when little comforts are offered to win over your allegiance. The most unfortunate result is collaborating with the same situation that tormented you previously.

In their journey out of Egypt, as recorded in Exodus 17, the Israelites kept on persuading Moses to return them back to their slave drivers. Their nostalgic appetites herding them back. Their fondest memories relived by the constant reminiscence of the Egyptian's diet- tales of the onions and garlic savored in slavery.

They grew so vulnerable, wearied by their memories. Their aspirations presented a complete paradigm from their initial hopes as slaves. They that previously hated Egypt with a passion felt a little more tolerant of it.

In God's master plan, the destination of choice was the Promised Land flowing with milk and honey- and not garlic and onions. In God's plan, the ultimate duty was delivering his nation from bondage and giving them an inheritance. This plan however suffered when the Israelites became troublesome and adopted the 'It is better the devil you know than the angel you don't' philosophy. To succeed, one thing must stand out- and that is to put aside the pleasures of the moment, and face the glorious eve of your vacation.

In His command to Abraham, God's instructions were similar- to get moving, and depart from the Chaldeans, who were his kinsmen, to the land of promise.

Very often, we chain ourselves to the same troubles because of little comforts. In the journey of life, no more attention than is necessary should be given to the pleasures of the moment at the expense of a much brighter destination.

The opportunity of reminiscence should never be lavished on the not-so-lovely status quo. However much you think about it, it remains status quo.

At the instance when you get fed-up and need to move, dial next. Whenever your reasons for progress outweigh the ones to remain, pack your bags and hit the track. Otherwise, by the mere act of looking back, you may end up as a pillar of salt.

It may seem propitious to remain in perpetual silence because of a little complacency here and there. Some lunch program, a bit of team building and before long, the opportunity is gone altogether. It often pays to keep moving towards your destination of choice. Remember, there is no time to sympathize with your tribulations.

Glancing temporarily at your rear view mirror might offer you an ideal opportunity to grin at your past mistakes. You must nevertheless steady your feet on the gas to seize your ultimate goals.

Your tormentor may put up a cunning face of appeal, so much so that moving on becomes your biggest hurdle. These attractions often come just after you have been handed down your choicest of tribulations.

To keep moving, you must learn to ease bonds and ties. Some of the times though, this would roll a tear down your chin and weariness through your heart. In spite of all these hurdles, you must keep going and learn to hold strong. Get your bags ready, journey arranged, and start moving toward success!

REMEMBER

- There is nothing as intricate as breaking loose
- The only way out of indecision is a bold step called detachment
- It takes stepping out to realize success
- There is never a perfect moment like here and now
- Initiative is the sole convener of coincidence
- To keep moving, you must ease bonds and free ties

CHAPTER 6

Soak Up Determination

Have you once failed and yet felt the nerve to proceed? How about being barred yet still holding out for a favorable ruling? How often have you been deprived, yet stayed on and on and on? Determination is that fuel that keeps the fire burning, and the flames licking even when the odds are evidently imposing.

Motivational stories are usually littered with streaks of determination which make them read like fairy tales, featuring clear shifts in paradigms and joints. Determination is the number one impetus that transforms a chump into champ and fires one from loser to winner.

Some glitches may appear but should never present real hindrances that impede progress. Not even age. Incredible as it may sound, age is only a juxtaposition of digits which mean little in the arena of achievement.

Determination is often wheeled by the means of trolleys called hope. And hope is a therapeutic deposit- a composite of the persona of those who haven't achieved, yet have a deep seated determination to continue in spite of it. Determination is the hope that keeps the never-do-wells from an attempt at their lives.

Hope is the persuasion to face another day with its struggles and challenges. It keeps determination alive and makes its adherents anticipate a better turn of events. It is that kind of determination that brings about a change of status and presents a chance to dream a better future in spite of a horrid present.

It is this strong conviction that there's a chance of achieving within a life time - a persuasion that there's only too little to die for. This is what inspires true determination.

REMEMBER

- ✦ Determination is the fuel that keeps the fire burning
- ✦ Determination is often wheeled upon trolleys of hope
- ✦ Determination is the hope that keeps the never-do-wells from an attempt at their lives
- ✦ Determination is the persuasion that there is only too little to die for

Believe in you

> "And he said unto him, Arise, go your
> way: your faith has made you whole"
>> (Luk 17: 19 KJV 2000)

Belief is a firm, audacious conviction revolving around a supposition. It is a strong positive feeling about an impression or sentiment. More synonymous with faith, it is what the scriptures in Hebrews 11 refer to as 'the substance of things hoped for and the evidence of things not seen'. The things we hold as true may not be forthright to everyone at the moment. In fact, they might not have a physical manifestation at all.

As a matter of fact, belief is a personal conviction that draws more from an inner view point. You have heard a popular creed that presupposes that to see is to believe. This philosophy seeks to compel our antennas to the popular view and eventually silence our novelty. The world nonetheless is slowly but surely realizing that believing is seeing.

Belief shapes with attitude retrospection. It is the truest genesis of hope and results. It has been said, 'attitude is altitude'. In other words, we may only scale to as high as we are able to see. In the true sense of the word, our sights clearly determine our heights.

It is impossible to possess what you are ignorant about. When God spoke to Abraham as recorded in the Bible in Genesis 13, He ordered him to lift up his eyes north, south, east and westward. Apparently, his entitlement for possession was limited to all the land he was able to see.

Our vision is certain to become blurred by the numerous insurmountable challenges that buffet us daily and the copious tears that drench our beliefs into surrender. In the end, it doesn't matter whether or not we shed tears. Moreover, whether our tears be tears of joy or sadness is neither here nor there. I shed tears, no doubt. My resolve has however changed. Presently, I have allowed my tears to moisten my eyes for an even clearer vision. The kind of vision that is essential.

The power of belief is borne in vision, the seed of which germinates into an undeniable fervor that transforms doubters into adherents.

There are potential greats out there who shoot themselves in the foot, more often by their statements of insurrection. Statements such as; 'I am not adequate for this task.' 'No matter what I do, I can't just get it right.' 'I must be the dumbest kid in my grade' and many more defeatist admissions. Beware! It is easy to destroy our most valued inner potentials by our statements of defeat. Every moment you confess inability, you have essentially deprived the muscle of capability.

Between each of our strides lie two possibilities; inability and capability. Often times, disability is misconstrued for inability. The former is only a physical disposition and doesn't carry the 'I am worthless' label.

On the contrary, inability is a kind of resignation which in spite of the God-given talents, focuses on a 'wait-for-the-manna-to-fall' attitude. There are those who have unfortunately fashioned their disabilities as an excuse for their inabilities. Inability of any kind must never be allowed to form a hindrance to progress. Keep moving, no matter what!

'Yes! We can!' A creed fashioned by Barack Obama in his grand march to White house in 2008 was a perfect display of faith. It demonstrated conviction. It is that same conviction that earned him a place as the first ever black president of the United States of America.

His shot at White house imbibed this psychological boost called conviction, propelling him all the way. It did little the fact that he was of an African vintage- a minority grouping in the US. His father having been Kenyan, and mother American was just the right ingredient for doubt.

What is hitherto apparent was that no amount of qualms sealed Barack's fate.

To Barack, possibility was such a real word and a product of an unwavering spirit. Backed by a prior failure for Congress, he still thrust himself into contention for the Democratic Party ticket against established names like Hilary Clinton.

There is nothing more unnerving than listening to negatives and the viewpoint of the surrendered. Remember, the body shape of the bumble bee renders it an aerodynamic impossibility. But it flies anyway since nobody told it that it can't fly.

There is one interesting story that I often recap to folks who'd care to consider. It is a story about my own encounter with self belief– one that has never escaped my conscience since. It is an account of how my math grades turned for the better during my last lap of high school.

When I joined High School, and progressing well, I sustained an appeal in languages and art. Unfortunately for me, my grades for math plummeted and the nerves for improvement numbed. Any comeback effort I set up got utterly bankrupt, and I couldn't improve whatsoever.

As was customary, the District mock results were promptly pinned on the notice board for all to behold. Nerves cracked, fingers itched and an aura of panic engulfed the candidates. The sight of stupefied students trooping to the notice-board to get a glance of the results was by now routine.

Reasons for glancing at the results weren't obvious among the ranks and files. My reason was to confirm that my grades remained stellar in arts and languages, and also to make sure they didn't plunge any further in math.

With my eyes glued to the notice board, I overheard a comment- not so common, and from a not so common student 'analyst'. Probably a first grader- I wasn't quite able to identify him. The comment set in me a huge psychological impact that needs no melodramatic elaboration. It gave me impetus to attain a lot more.

I owe that lone student a lot for raising my confidence and purging my difficulty in Math. I had made a dismal grade in Math and it's what prompted the comment. 'What a feat! How could this candidate rank among the top with grade 'D' in Math, whereas everybody else in top ten scored anything but 'B' or 'A'?', 'Now, supposing he scored 'B', wouldn't it impact his overall performance by leaps and bounds?' the unfamiliar voice rested those fond submissions.

To me, those were reasons enough to test the hypothesis and find out what impact it could have had on my grade. Any claim that my confidence level improved is an understatement. Truth is, I walked to my Math teacher and made that famous commitment to score no other grade, but 'A' in Math. That was the degree of certainty that made me overhaul my performance in Math, and made me score 'A' in Math. I soon found out that the ability was in borne, yet waiting for an opportunity of self belief.

Everyone has a dynamic ability that revolves around self-belief. This ability is perennially waiting for your summonses to get it out. Make sure to identify the cause of your continued derailment lest these detractors dwarf your rhythm for success. Wake up and spring forth, for this is the right time to make good your onslaught.

The practice of exercising self belief counts in every respect. Self belief is a feeling about self and can never be stumbled upon- it is earned by constant training. It is the life blood of courage. Whereas self belief is a feeling of self-worth, courage is its outward demonstration. It should never be misconstrued for arrogance or mere bravado. Self belief is seen through the window of courage.

Some years back, I appeared for an interview at a consulting company. The firm, a building services Consultancy offered me an opportunity to demonstrate some fundamentals of electrical design and implementation. Prior to this, I worked as a projects' supervisor for a civil and construction company- an assignment which offered no electrical engineering experience, much less any technical know how.

Engineering designs demand a working knowledge of AutoCAD software for drafting computer aided designs, a good understanding of power distribution, cable sizing, standby generator sizing, and load calculations among other engineering computations.

Moreover, these designs must be backed by an accurate generation of a bill of quantities to capture the project in its entirety. Other requirements during this design process would be project implementation and supervision.

Strikingly though, our syllabi gave these concepts a wide berth and assumed they are worth acquiring elsewhere. I don't deny that students must initiate responsibility to learn on their own, apart from the guidance received from faculty. However, when I appeared before Engineer Aruna Patel, none of these counted the least. What she required was my assurances to deliver assignments fast enough.

The quizzes were debilitating and nerve wrecking. I attempted to table certificates but 'no', she responded curtly. 'Are you able to do the job', she interrupted my thoughts with a resounding finality. 'Yes', I countered decisively. 'George! Get me an AutoCAD drawing!' she ordered and quickly passed it over to me. 'Here, show me precisely how to perform power and light designs and mind too the correct cable sizes', she interjected.

At this moment, there was every cause to be flummoxed or naturally spellbound. I had never taken a more considered view of a building plan prior to that, and this first opportunity rubbed me the wrong way. The more I tried to construct head or even tail of it, the more it dodged me. Fidgeting with the plan and tossing it back and forth did not help matters at all.

The plan was nothing akin to the engineering drawings in second year of campus. It wasn't comprehensible from my 'layman's perspective either. It wasn't ordinary apartments block drawing meant for demonstration nor was it a mere pullout from an architect's sketchpad. No, it was an actual design meant for implementation. My gaze remained transfixed on the drawing just figuring out how to frame my response. The pencil in my grip did not etch a mark on the drawing that stared at me all the while.

Apart from the obvious jinx and farce, I determined to put forth a strong case for myself. Whenever I hit a snag, my reassurances were avid and adept and quite frankly quick to the rescue. In the end, it didn't matter whether I knew an Iota or not, what was important to me is that I got the job.

'Ma'am, my propensity to build on new knowledge remains the single most given', I often reiterated. 'And please, just allow me to give you my word on this', I proceeded, 'I will never disappoint your faith in me, if you allow me to have it', and so I concluded.

I briskly summoned the people-person enthusiasm during the entire conversation. Somehow, I drew the urge learnt that even in technical lines success is pegged on personality and the ability to lead people.

'Alright Patrick, let me observe you for a month', she concluded. As you can see, I had effectively worked my strengths to neutralize my weaknesses and by virtue of my self belief I earned her trust.

Self belief is the one solemn germ of enthusiasm that arouses an intense exuberance. It remains the single most important tool that every leader requires in dealing with people. And according to John D. Rockefeller, the ability to deal with people is as purchasable a commodity as sugar or coffee, and he'd pay more for that ability, than for any other under the sun.

REMEMBER

- ⊕ Belief is a firm, audacious conviction revolving around a supposition
- ⊕ Belief shapes up with attitude retrospection
- ⊕ It is impossible to possess what you're ignorant about
- ⊕ Between each of our strides lie two possibilities; Inability and capability
- ⊕ There's nothing more unnerving than listening to the negatives and viewpoints of the resigned
- ⊕ Everyone has a dynamism that revolves around self-belief
- ⊕ Self belief is never stumbled upon, it is earned by constant training

Be consistent

Whereas both continuity and consistency are singularly and jointly important, they are not one and the same thing. Consistency, also referred to as coherence shouldn't be misconstrued for continuity. Whereas consistency is a quality of remaining unchanged over time, continuity denotes a non –ending cycle.

It is obvious that actions- good or otherwise repeated, have a natural ability of firming up to create the effect popularly referred to as experience. So, the more you practice a concept the more you gain currency and confidence in it. It has been emphasized before that practice makes perfect. And this is the genius of persistence that exposes the underbelly of failure.

Just like pressing a creased cloth with a continuous passing of pressure and heat, so it is with the human intellect.

For students, it is proper to know that studying demands going over a study material over and over, what is otherwise referred to as revision. A mere dab only makes for familiarity.

Sometimes, you just might be branded a dunce for going over the same materials again. Take no offence. More importantly, you're never going to remain the same half-witted, clumsy goose for going over it again. Fact is, you did learn a thing or two and made new discoveries.

Remember, practice makes perfect sense. Genius is a result of constant practice that issues from a pattern of consistency. The moment you develop a culture, it becomes difficult to move away from it.

Success therefore is not a one time occurrence, but a lifestyle achieved by a consistent fuel called practice. The fuel of success is practice and must be done throughout.

One feature of consistency is adaptation. It is characterized by an acquisition of traits which incidentally increases the suitability for a particular function. Any muscle constantly exercised invariably grows larger. This too applies to behavior. The moment you regularize an activity, it ceases to be a dull, futile exercise but instantly transforms into a seamless way of life.

REMEMBER

- ✦ Repeated actions, good or otherwise have a natural ability of creating an effect called experience
- ✦ Practice makes real and perfect sense
- ✦ Success is not a one term occurrence, but a lifestyle achieved by a constant fuel called practice
- ✦ One feature of consistency is adaptation
- ✦ A regularized activity transforms into a seamless way of life

Take the risk

> "Be strong and of a good courage, fear
> not, nor be afraid of them: for the LORD
> your God, he it is that does go with you;
> he will not fail you, nor forsake you"
>
> (Deut 31:6 KJV 2000)

To risk is to adventure. Everybody loves adventure but just a few would choose to risk it if ever. World over, the continued obsession for adventure has flourished several careers and sponsored great films. 'National geographic' and a lot more of other documentaries and films have been made for the cause of adventure. Most discoveries are adventure borne and it could well be said that discoveries are cause for adventure.

Anytime you adventure out, you most likely will get a result. Like the West African cocoa, most products sprout out of adventure.

United States of America was discovered by Christopher Columbus when his love for adventure drove him to explore new sights. Those who abhor adventure will less likely know whether their attempts could have borne fruits.

Adventure has a characteristic feature- constant change, adaptability and a knack for new ways. It is the adventurous mind that wanders and journeys towards discovery. The realization that failure excels in exposing the ways that do not work should be our number one driving philosophy.

The love for adventure is the reason young kids jostle for the front seats in cars and align with their bus windows. Growing up, I picked the habit of securing window seats or the seats at the front of vehicles. Some of the times, I gobbled down breakfast as a plan to take up my position early enough. After all, it was no use squabbling over a mere seating position.

When I joined high school, I discovered that several others students had this same knack for front seats and window opportunities. When campus came knocking, the same prodding resurfaced albeit with a little laxity.

Over the years, I have ceased this push and shove. However, I have noticed this same habit among my little cousins whenever I drive them around. This probably explains why the 'window' has an obvious connotation when referencing to opportunity.

Most of the times, doors remain locked and are hardly ever designed as see through. On the contrary, windows remain open through the day or at least offer transparence through their clear glass panes.

I did not quite fathom the actual dimensions of grabbing opportunities- not until I examined the account of the lepers at the entrance of besieged Samaria. From that authentic Bible account, it became pretty obvious that taking a risk is something akin to entreating danger.

In the Bible, the seventh Chapter of second Kings unveils the story of some four lepers banished for their impurity- apparently due to their leprous affliction. This condition, considered defiling kept the lepers languished in isolation and biting famine. So horrid was the famine that a donkey's head was sought for food.

The conversation among the lepers should be significantly thought-out and here is the transcript. "If we say, We will enter into the city, then the famine is in the city, and we shall die there: and if we sit still here, we die also. Now therefore come, and let us fall unto the army of the Syrians: if they save us alive, we shall live; and if they kill us, we shall but die" (2 Kings 7:4-5 KJV 2000)

As twilight drew closer, the lepers advanced toward the Syrian camp. To their bewilderment, the Syrian camp was eerily abandoned yet filled with food, drink and an assortment of fine resources.

Sitting at their previous isolation zones carried a death penalty slowly advancing. Heading for the besieged Samaria carried a definite death penalty, with no chance for survival. Going to the enemy camp was sufficient invitation for danger and they knew it very well. However, it was the only option with two alternatives; death or possibility life.

In the pursuit of success, we must be ready for the risks. By walking, we must tread the uncharted course and sail the unfamiliar waters. Taking a risk consists of exercising bravery and most often, it will meet a lot of negativity.

There is no shorter way to plain and ordinary living except by no longer risking. You must determine to get out of the waiting bay and proceed into the doctor's room. Take up the challenge head on.

Once during a students' challenge programme at YMCA Nairobi, I charged participants to consider why challenges are never meticulous. Several proposals were fronted by the students, and every reason pointed to the attendant risks associated with the challenges.

Challenges are risky and can never be handled meticulously. They are often flung around, and only the daring take them down. You will however hear numerous reasons why it's too risky, or why that's pushing too far and why we won't quite take the step.

REMEMBER

- To risk is to adventure
- Adventure has a characteristic feature called constant change, adaptability and a knack for new ways
- In the pursuit of success, we must be ready for the risks
- There's no shorter way to plain and ordinary living except in no longer risking
- Challenges are risky and can never be handled meticulously

Take stock and Plan your onslaught

Life is a journey into the unexplored jungle. Such journeys must be subjected to routine examination, planning and stock taking. A map is a kind of plan with pointers for directions, routes, distances and other essentials which give navigation aid for the unexplored terrain.

Our journeys take us to diverse jungles and everybody must keep their plans in constant check.

My first week on campus was both spectacular and breathtaking. I had earlier on been admitted to Kenyatta University. Soon after, the institution experienced a troublesome orientation marred by student riots due to fee increment. The skirmishes brought to a standstill operations at the main campus.

During this chaotic period, I made a switch to Nairobi University's College of Architecture and Engineering. The commencement date was set two months away from when Kenyatta University opened its gates for freshmen.

Registration is usually a daylong exercise and snaking queues wouldn't be surprising at all. By noon, 'CELT' registration desk was now recording fewer visits for enquiries and directions.

By evening, hostel rooms had been allocated and it was now pretty obvious that I was destined to spend my first night in one of the prefabricated hostels. Prefab '5 room 7' was my room for that year. 'Mamlaka A' was the towering concrete hostel overlooking our prefab and four more prefab blocks.

Mamlaka hostel housed senior engineering students, and it was evidently apparent from how its residents carried out themselves on campus. As a freshman, five years seemed indomitable. How could 1,825 days dawn and dusk before campus is declared done with? That kind of imagination was improbable.

The imposing time mountain ahead was such a colossal bridge to surmount. In no time, I had conveniently pinned a calendar on my wall, from which point I began to cross each day as it passed. The daily cancellation routine became a dull exercise and before I knew it, I had actually stopped the practice. I then started checking out months, which I ceased as well. Finally, I checked out my first year and in no time, college was no more.

Counting downwards is a stock taking practice with a strong psychological ramification. It thrives on the justification that the end is always nearer than the actual point of commencement. In the gym, exertions are often counted downwards as a way of motivating the psyche. You will no doubt realize that counting 4, 3, 2, 1, 0 is often psyche relieving than counting 0, 1, 2, 3, 4.

Whether you refer to time, weight, length, or any other measurement parameters, 10 presents a momentous challenge compared to 1. 10 appears further compared to 1, 10 appears weightier compared to 1, 10 appears longer compared to 1. In essence, counting down presents a feeling of winding down and keeps the spirit alive throughout your present challenge.

A plan orders the succession of events and refreshes the mind. Failure to plan is a clear invitation of failure. This is because everything jumbles up in the haphazard haze and no room is left for sobriety.

A plan, whether meticulous or not should address such questions as; what ideally should be accomplished in the next hour? What is the average time required to complete this current assignment? What must come at the tail end of my current undertaking? What amount of attention is needed by this present engagement? What is the likelihood that the current activity will roll beyond the stipulated time? All these constellation of questions clears the mental jam and removes any chance for indecision.

It is quite in order to gauge tasks and allocate time to each, proportional to their fair demands. It is nonetheless critical to take utmost caution that not all the time is allocated toward planning. Otherwise, the plan itself eats into the limited time resources available. Key, plan and move!

Every decision made should be backed up by a plan, irrespective of its magnitude. A decision is a very central aspect of life. It is a key component of the very human nature. Most importantly, get into a position of taking up choices and making good decisions.

REMEMBER

- Life is a journey into the unexplored jungle
- A plan guides the progression of events and refreshes the mind
- Every decision made, irrespective of magnitude should be backed up by a plan

PATRICK OTUOMA

Patrick Otuoma holds a B.Sc in Electrical Engineering from the University of Nairobi. He is currently undertaking a Masters of Arts in Projects Planning and Management at the same university. Apart from his engineering practice, the author has continually given motivational talks and lectures to students and various work groups across East Africa.